Ethical Investment
What is the way forward?

Ellen Teague

Published by Redemptorist Publications
Copyright © 2001 Redemptorist Publications
A Registered Charity

Text: Ellen Teague
Cover: Amanda Lillywhite
UK edition July 2001

All rights reserved. No part of this publication may be reproduced, or transmitted in any form or by any means, electronic or mechanical, including photocopying, recording, or by any information storage or retrieval system, without permission in writing from the publishers.

This book is sold subject to the conditions that it shall not be lent, resold, hired out or otherwise circulated without the publishers prior consent in any form other than which it is published.

ISBN 085231 243 1

Redemptorist
PUBLICATIONS

Alphonsus House Chawton Hampshire GU34 3HQ
Telephone 01420 88222   Fax 01420 88805
rp@redempt.org   www.redempt.org

Contents:

What is Ethical Investment	5
Criteria for Ethical Investment	6
Ethical Banking	7
Triodos Bank	8
Shared Interest	9
Other Ethical Banking Services	11
Ethical Financial Planning	12
EIRIS	13
The Ethical Investment Consultancy	14

Using your money to build a better world

What is ethical investment?

When people make important decisions in their lives, they act in accordance with their values and beliefs. By investing in a socially and environmentally responsible manner, money can be used to work towards a more just and environmentally sustainable society, as well as meeting personal financial needs. Unless a conscious decision is made to make an ethical option, investment may well be in companies whose products and services we may disagree with.

Ethical investment can mean a refusal to invest in or to withdraw investment from particular companies or banks. Recent research has shown that investors usually have concerns about a range of issues rather than just one or two. People who care about tobacco products, for example, will typically be concerned about the arms trade or nuclear energy as well. They will probably care greatly about social and economic inequality in the UK and Europe as well as Third World poverty.

Ethical investment can be a positive choice of investments on the basis of good employment practices such as equal opportunities, concern for the environment, an anti-pollution policy, or local community involvement.

Criteria for ethical investment

The following investment areas are amongst those normally avoided by those applying ethical criteria:

Armaments – The production, supply, or offer to supply, of weapons and their components.

Mines and Plantations – The operation in countries of the South of mines or plantations unless they are clearly found not to be unjustly exploiting the labour force or the local environment.

Banks involved in Third World Debt – Involvement in extracting money from already impoverished countries and in the form of interest payments.

Sex Industry – Production of pornographic materials or media presentations demeaning the transcendent dignity of the human person.

Abortion – Companies involved in supporting and

promoting abortion and the production of abortifacient materials.

Other issues worthy of consideration might be: gambling, alcohol, animal-testing, advertising, donations to political parties and transnationals.

Ethical Banking

Most people rely on bank accounts when it comes to organising their day-to-day finances. A number of institutions now offer banking services to customers concerned about ethical issues. The Co-operative Bank, for example, has had an ethical policy since 1992, which governs how customers' money should and should not be invested. This covers human rights, arms, fair trading, ecological impact and animal welfare. Building societies can also provide banking services. Some ethical investors prefer them to high street banks because of their mutual status and because most of their business comes from lending on homes and not from international banking services. The Ecology Building Society, for example, promotes sustainable housing and communities and in addition offers a range of savings accounts and mortgages.

Triodos Bank

The Triodos Bank invests only in organisations and businesses with social and environmental objectives. A range of accounts are offered and some target specific areas for investment such as housing, renewable energy and organic agriculture. Founded in the Netherlands in 1980, the bank came to the UK in 1995 where it has doubled in size every 12 months, with customers all over the country. Its principles and independence are guaranteed through a trust which holds all the shares and protects the social and environmental aims of the bank. The Triodos Bank is closely regulated by the Dutch Central Bank and the Bank of England. All members of the European Union now have banking legislation to meet the same minimum standards for deposit protection, which means that savings in Triodos Bank receive the same level of protection as they would with any UK bank.

Accounts can be set up and accessed at high street banks or by correspondence direct with Triodos. Interest rates are comparable and in many cases better than high street banks. Savings accounts are usually run free of charge and there is no fee for normal deposits, withdrawals, account statements or tax certificates.

Contact: Triodos Bank, Brunel House, 11 The Promenade, Clifton, Bristol BS8 3NN
Tel: freephone 0500 008 720
e-mail: mail@triodos.co.uk
http://www.triodos.co.uk

Shared Interest

Shoppers may have noticed an increasingly familiar brand of coffee on their local supermarket shelves. It is a good quality freeze dried coffee similar to the leading brands, but it is a coffee with a difference. Called Cafédirect it is the first 'fairly traded' coffee to be sold in UK supermarkets. This means that co-operatives of coffee farmers in the Third World get a fair price for their coffee from Alternative Trade Organisations such as Traidcraft, Oxfam Trading and *Cafédirect*. One of the coffee farmers in Peru, Jose Rivera Campoverde explains what this has meant to him and other farmers "Our co-operative can afford to pay a doctor who will give treatment to our members. For myself, the price difference has meant I can afford more food for my family and to send my children to school properly equipped with pens and notebooks for the first time".

The move towards fair trade can be supported not

just by drinking Cafédirect coffee but also by lending your savings to Third World producers of coffee and other items through an organisation in this country called "Shared Interest." Managing Director of Shared Interest, Stephanie Sturrock, explains: "One of the major obstacles for Third World producers is that they have insufficient capital and often cannot get loans from local banks. We offer people in this country the opportunity to lend their savings to these producers on fair terms. It is not charity, but a partnership, based on mutual trust and respect. They have the skills and commitment to make their enterprises succeed and we demonstrate our belief in them through the loans we make."

Shared Interest is a co-operative lending society with around 8,500 members. Members are aware of the problems faced by producers in the Third World in getting access to credit and they are willing to invest part of their savings in order to help producers pay for the costs of producing their goods until the goods can be sold to consumers. Established in 1990, Shared Interest has grown rapidly and has reached a total share capital of £16 million. It is very like a lending co-operative. Investors become members and can open an account with £100 (£20,000 maximum). Their money earns interest and can normally be withdrawn whenever they want it, by return of post.

Contact: Shared Interest Society Ltd,
25 Collingwood St, Newcastle Upon Tyne,
Tyne And Wear, NE1 1JE
New membership enquiries: 0191 2339101
e-mail: post@shared-interest.com
http://www.shared-interest.com

Other Ethical Banking Services:

Co-operative Bank, PO Box 101, 1 Balloon Street, Manchester M60 4EP. Tel: 0800 905 090

Ecology Building Society, 18 Station Road, Crosshills, Keighley BD20 7EH. Tel: 01535 635933.

Norwich and Peterborough Building Society (offers green mortgages) Tel: 0800 883 322.

Credit Unions are not designed specifically for ethical or environmentally-conscious investors, but their role as non-profit-making community organisations providing low-cost loans make them a popular choice for people who want to make their finances more ethical.

The Association of British Credit Unions can be reached on 0161 832 3694.

Ethical Financial Planning

Five things you can do:
1. If you're putting away savings regularly, think about putting some of them into an ethical investment fund.
2. If you have a personal pension, transfer your contributions to one of the ethical funds. Many ethical investment funds can be used for this, or for paying in Additional Voluntary Contributions (AVCs).
3. Think about moving your current bank account to a provider known for its strong ethical policies.
4. If you invest in gilts, bear in mind that the government will use your money to finance a wide variety of public spending. This will include defence, as well as health and education. Consider the public good that your money will be put to balanced against the issues that concern you.
5. Consider moving your car insurance to a provider with a track record of sound ethical policies. Providers include the Environmental

Transport Association, which does not lobby for more roads.

EIRIS

The Ethical Investment Research Service (EIRIS) was set up in 1983 with the help of churches and charities which had investments and needed a research organisation to help them put their principles into practice. It provides independent research into corporate behaviour needed by ethical investors. EIRIS helps charities and other investors identify the approach appropriate to their requirements and publishes guides to help investors and advisers identify and choose between funds with ethical criteria. It has a database on over 1,000 UK and 500 European companies and uses 200 ethical performance indicators. Individual investors are enabled to create a portfolio that reflects their own ethical concerns.

Contact: EIRIS, 80-84 Bondway, London SW8 1SF. For a list of independent financial advisors phone 0845 606 0324

General information packs on ethical investment are available from 0845 606 0324

Share screening and other services for ethical investors available from 020 7840 570

The Ethical Investor (bi-monthly newsletter, £15 per year) from 020 7840 5700

The Ethical Investment Consultancy

This offers professional advice from specialist in ethical investment, Greg McCrave, who has advised charities, Catholic groups and dioceses. A pack of information can be sent on request. Financial planning areas include: mortgages, pensions, savings and investments, life assurance, income protection, long term care and estate protection.

Contact: The Ethical Investment Consultancy,
St. Walburge's Centre, St. Walburge's Gardens,
Preston PR2 2QJ
Tel/fax: 01772 733338
Internet: www.profitwithprinciple.co.uk

Did you know?

- Catholic dioceses and religious orders have been disinvesting in the arms industry over recent years and in companies such as British Aerospace.

- The average UK ethical investment fund has grown by almost 29% over the last year. There are a growing number of ethical options - for students opening their first bank account or a retiring professional with a lump sum to invest.

- The Diana, Princess of Wales Memorial Fund has an ethical policy for its £72 million of investments. None will be invested in companies where more than five per cent of sales come from tobacco or arms.

Investor Profile

Edward, a water industry consultant from Swindon in his fifties, has a total of £60,000 invested according to ethical criteria for his children's university education. The decision to invest ethically was made earlier in life, when he was teaching mathematics and statistics in Pakistan. He says, "I realised then that life can be very difficult for some people, and how the action of big companies could make a difference one way or the other." He avoids drug and armaments companies that "dump products in the Third World which do not pass regulations in the US and Britain." He also tries to avoid companies that market baby milk in the Third World. Edward has a "couple of thousand pounds" in Shared Interest and also holds a Just Housing Account from Triodos Bank. He has an ethical TESSA and a PEP. His current account is with one of the demutualised building societies.

> **The Catechism of the Catholic Church says:** "In place of abusive if not usurious financial systems, iniquitous commercial relations between nations, and the arms race, there must be substituted a common effort to mobilise resources towards objectives of moral, cultural and economic development, redefining the priorities and hierarchies of values." (2438)

Look up:
Luke 19:8-9 and Acts 4:34-37
What do these passages tell us about a Christian perspective on money?